Signal Moments

Poems of Loss and an Antidote

Marilyn Kiss

Plain View Press
P. O. 42255
Austin, TX 78704

plainviewpress.net
sb@plainviewpress.net
1-512-441-2452

Copyright Marilyn Kiss, 2007. All rights reserved.
ISBN: 978-1-891386-91-6
Library of Congress Number: 2007936799

Cover photo, *Railroad Crossing*, ©, 2007, Wilson Tsoi
Author photo by Miguel Angel.

Acknowledgments

"In Memoriam: Octavia Butler (1947-2006)." *Nimbus*. NY: The Print Center, Fall, 2006 (28); "Chilean Obituary: The Other September 11 (for Pedro Pietri)." *Nimbus*. NY: The Print Center, Fall, 2005 (18); "In Memoriam: Edward Said and "The Corrida." *Nimbus*. NY: The Print Center, Spring, 2004 (11, 19); "Carolyn G. Heilbrun: Dead at Age 77." *Nimbus*. NY: The Print Center, Fall, 2003 (52); "Joe Strummer: 1952-2002." *Nimbus*. NY: The Print Center, Spring, 2003 (76-77); " On a clear day…," "Icarus, September 12" and "Islands." *Nimbus*. NY: The Print Center, Fall, 2001 (48-52); "In Memoriam: Janis Joplin, October 4, 1970" and "In Memoriam: Pablo Neruda, October, 1973." *Nimbus*. NY: The Print Center, Fall, 2000 (35-38); "Self-hatred" and "Mother: A.D." *Long Shot*, Vol. 15. Hoboken, NJ: Long Shot Publications, Fall, 1993 (154-155); "Posthumous Kisses." *A Poetry Collection*. NY: NYU/FRN, 1991 (11); "Passion as…." *The Journal of New Jersey Poets*, Vol. VII, No. 1. Madison, NJ: 1985 (34-35); "Poem as…" *The Hoboken Terminal*. NJ: Little Father Time Society, 1983 (64-65); "Cats." *Anthologist*, Spring, Vol. II. New Brunswick, NJ: Rutgers U, 1974 (49).

Sincere thanks to Susan Bright, Bob Holman, Nancy Mercado, Renny Molenaar, Ernesto Ballesteros (QEPD), Desiree Braithwaite, and the Wagner College FRF. A Miguel Angel, mis gracias y mucho amor.

Contents

Foreword	7
First Moment: 7:31 a.m.	9
Posthumous Kisses	11
Mother, A.D.	12
In My Mother's Drawers	13
On Changing My Mother's Diapers	14
To Be	15
Lullaby	16
Death Poem From a Daughter	17
Contractions	18
The Gloaming	21
The Corrida	23
Conception Scene	24
Granddaddy Daddy	25
Admonition	26
Self-hatred	27
Rag Rug	28
Panther	29
Niece No More	30
Second Moment: 8:20 p.m.	31
Accident	33
Semi-Sacrifice	34
X-Ray	36
Portrait	37
Third Moment: 11:31 p.m.	39
Giza's Art	41
Giza's Studio	43
The House Across the River	45
Of Fragile, Delicate Creatures	46
Invasions, 1991	47
The Dance	48
The way it was w'posed to be	49

Fourth Moment: 5:34 p.m.   51

    Inter-species   53
    On Driving My Dog To His Execution   54
    Doggie At the Window   55
    My Imaginary Friend   56
    Foto: April 1, 1994 – January 6, 2007   57

Fifth Moment: 6:00 a.m.   59

    In Memoriam: Janis Joplin, October 4, 1970   61
    In Memoriam: Pablo Neruda, October 1973   62
    In Memoriam: Joe Strummer: 1952-2002   64
    Carolyn G. Heilbrun: Dead at Age 77   67
    In Memoriam: Edward Said: 1935-2003   69
    In Memoriam: Octavia Butler: 1947-2006   71
    Hiroshima: Exculpation   72
    Chilean Obituary: The Other September 11   73
    On a Clear Day…   76
    Icarus, September 12   78
    Islands   79
    Memorial, March 2002   80
    When? 2007   81

Sixth Moment: 3:10 a.m.   83

    Poem as…..   85
    Cats   88
    My Voice   90
    Passion As…   91
    Poem Without Face   93
    Pastime   94
    Nocturne   95
    Photography As…   96
    Visitation   97
    Habitat   98
    Sailing To You….   99

    About the Author   101

Dedication:

For **Katie** (1904-1989) and **Henry** (1890-1976)

Foreword

The 900 inhabitants of La Plata, Missouri, had their days divided by shrill whistles: the 7:00 a.m. wake-up call; the noon and 1:00 p.m. lunch break parentheses; the 5:00 p.m. signal for quitting time. Years after the natural gas pipeline was laid and the workers scattered, the acoustic reminders of the project still remained.

For my 5-year-old self, it was the day's final whistle that was most important since it meant my father would soon be home to take me to the Santa Fe railroad station to watch the 5:20 Zephyr breeze by. My tiny hand in his large one, I began dreaming of distant places. This daily event was one I treasured.

Not all of life's transformative moments, however, are so pleasant; nor are they announced by such an audible marker.

First Moment:

7:31 a.m.

Posthumous Kisses

We joked, she and I
of some basic bifurcation
some maternal process
which sent us
to divergent tactics,
a duality of solutions.

Take make-up:

my lipstick colors
opposite the spectrum
from hers
my wands pointed
from routines
of a different order
hers, flat mesas
of habit and application

Now I use her leftovers,
smearing my mouth
mauve shimmer
dusty pink, heather rose
peach haze, tender berry
seeking a touch, a
warmth, a contact

yearning for comfort,
for release from sorrow,
for surcease,
wanting to bypass the grief,
to bridge the gulf,
desiring a kiss
from beyond the grave.

Mother, A.D.

In my dream of her
    she rides a horse
hair flying like a replicated mane
    she wears a purple cloak
of indigo hue mixed with blood
    she speeds with the wind
even though the dream
is black and white
even though in life
no hair was ever unpinned
no scarf ever untucked
no quest so unlicensed

In my dream of her
    she is a mare
    she is a rainbow
    she is a zephyr

In my dream of her
    in black and white
she is breathless
the clouds of her rapid respiration
like bright halos
above her quick steed
her regal raiment

In my dream of her
she is not dead.

In My Mother's Drawers

Exploration began
and ended
in my mother's drawers
the satin lingerie
of childhood fantasy
the cedar protection
of adult reality
the missing links
imagined between the
voices of past and present
of joy and indifference
of curse and realization

The perfumed capsules
an open invitation to
introspection
the texture of mystery

the pull of worlds
to be opened like drawers

the strength of gravity
against the wood of drawers

my skin in lace
in drawers

On Changing My Mother's Diapers

Incontinence would be temporary,
or so they said,
those who should know such things,
those who study them.

You were barely there, almost invisible
rambling around in your own clothes
like a toddler playing dress-up,
flesh like a turkey's wattles
but only half as red,
so frighteningly tiny,
YOU, who had loomed so large.

You apologized profusely, embarrassed,
that years could do such damage,
angry that time was no longer on your side.

You peed, and that we dealt with,
ammonia pungency, acrid sting in the eyes.

It was when I really had to change you
that generational wheels ground to a halt,
that courses unchartered revealed themselves,
that something got caught in the blood,
that you vomited
and so did I.

To Be

Is the greater courage
living to the roots
of each gray hair,
every stony disillusionment,
suffering yet another arthritic joint?

No ovens to the head
to ease the clanging;
no Hemingway out
for those daring to
face arch enemies
raging through the veins.

Valor not in premeditated death or
valor in imitating Harold's Maude?

Who at eighty has not dreamed of
surcease yet who has not smiled at one more
holiday package?

The will sublime, the spirit flagging,
the corporeal reality fading yet persistent,
wrestling with Hamlet's over-cited question,
seeking bravery in existence.

Lullaby

Curled in maternal embrace
I believed that
"hush now, you sleepy
little sheep"
would always bring
the heavy eyelid,
the drooping head,
the dark curtain.

Nights prior to nostalgia
those voiceless sibilants
proffered surcease,
cessation,
succor.
Beyond belief or measure,
the arms, the lamb,
the story
held and beheld
the sacred passage.

The night hisses still.
Serpents crawl beneath the pillow,
lizards swirl in the legs
reeling to a call
unanswered.

Where now the lap,
the love,
the lethal dosage?

Death Poem From a Daughter

Your silence does not inhibit me
for I know the dialogue
as though from a distant memory
as old as motherhood itself.
Your answers, your postulations
have always been there,
suspended in proximity
as well as in distance,
tones
in the diametrics of space.
The uterine bonds we share
are a language
that breaks and breathes
on matriarchal shores
where spirits gather
to celebrate the very essence
of being.
The chords between us
are unbroken, the harmony
undiminished,
the melody uninterrupted.
We are one and two and
infinity you and I,
and thus it ever was.
The message is clear.
I hear you as I adore you,
unceasingly.

Contractions

(For my parents)

Contractions it's called
when the fluid pushes
and the blood begins.
The timing warps the universe
for those moments
as space coalesces
and then expands.
Concentric circles start their
outward spin.
The winding tunnel expels
through crimson into white,
from warmth to cries and cold.
The walls blanche,
the room wails,
reverberations echo.
Dilation, elation, relation.
Widening contacts form steps,
then words, then worlds.

Take notice of contractions.

Expansion it's called
as scholarship broadens
and experience takes root.
The joy rattles the perimeters
for those decades
as productivity increases
and students gather.
Abundant connections
make their timely appearance.
The acknowledged trail leads
from classroom to hearth,
from heartland to golden state,

from dream to fulfillment.
The chalk dust flies,
essays are corrected,
the verbs get conjugated.
Education, procreation, satisfaction.
Career advancements increase potential,
Then realization, then finalization.

Enjoy expansions.

Contractions it's called
when the ink dries
and bonds are formed.
The disillusionment stalls the spheres
for those periods
as cement hardens and joints stiffen.
Constricting spirals limit
the underlying intentions.
The narrow gauges of hope, then fear
change green to gray
and joy to abandon.
Time hovers,
veins burst, teeth decay,
goals screech to a halt.
Condemnation, stagnation, recrimination.
Fewer possibilities
dim dreams, then sight, then meaning.

Beware of contractions.

Contractions it's called
when friends die
and silence sets in.
The pain startles the planets
for those years
as god disappears

and death awaits.
Confusing elements
reap their daily harvest.
The awkward path meanders from
independence to need,
from continence to filth,
from reality to memory.
The stones keen,
flowers wilt,
the sod dries to dust.
Ossification, tribulation, isolation.
Converging forces weave tears,
then veils, then shrouds.

Accept contractions.

The Gloaming

Age came for my mother
when I was 23
full of myself and
high on Simone de Beauvoir.

I was there, a routine visit to the family home
late afternoon arrival
dust motes hanging on waning
rays of the October sun
angling through the starched lace curtains,
recently washed,
the light oblique across
mauve walls.

I was there when age ambushed my mother.
In the dining room, it was,
where framed verses
had always hung.

Stealthily, relentlessly age
crept up on my mother.

Quick movement, a resounding crash.
"Grow old along with me/
The best is yet to be"
vanished from above the
oak table, flew across
the hardwood floors, the hooked rug,
smashed into the sideboard
       shards of glass splintering
       poetry crumpling
       hope unraveling

"The last of life/for which the first was made"
       no longer as promising

        no longer anticipated
        no longer viable.

Age came for my mother
when I was 23.

Now it has come
for me.

The Corrida

Bugles, drums, fanfare!
A matador enters the ring
sand raked smooth, unlined
spotless before the contest,
an encounter as ancient
as Minoan Crete.

In our name, the bullfighter faces all fears, confronts death.

My bull is darkly ominous; it is age itself
charging through the veins
goring and gouging
a muscle here, an organ there.

I mold my sagging flesh
in satin and sequins, a suit of lights
                        and stubbornly shout, ¡Olé!

Conception Scene

I searched longingly for that tree
the roots of family mythology
the one that provided the
canopy
for my conception

A redwood tree, naturally
to match the size of my daddy's desire
the enormity of his ego to dream a daughter
at his age
The red/green a reflection of
the ripeness of my mother's womb
on hold for all those years
but wanting
yes aching
for the results
of a night spent
nestled on forest needles
snuggled in starlight
beneath that elusive tree.

Granddaddy Daddy

My tree trunk of a daddy
a granddaddy daddy
with hands so large they
could hold me in my
nude newness
to look at the world from his height

Old fool they called
him, his family
for siring a daughter
in those grandfatherly years
the waning decades
of adventure and bachelorhood

Out of his mind they said
of my granddaddy daddy
as we shopped for Cheerios
did bikes, then guns, then cars
explored dirt roads and river banks
kept secrets from my mother

Is that your granddaughter? Strangers asked
No, said proudly, a gleam in his eye
You have to be a father first

Admonition

Keep your knees together
my mother always said.

Rebellious, disobedient knees
locking around the bearded night
pale signposts of unshakeable solitude.

Obstinate, paradoxical knees
bowing before nothing
yet refusing confidence like
an alien garb.

Cowardly knees, closing in on ripe strawberries.
Brash knees, going to the groin in violent protection.
A geometry of knees for country and city
ridiculous and scarred by desires.

Can these knees belong to me,
glued on like bonnets
to lean appendages,
meager skills?

What do I see but a mirror full of knees,
twice-told, redundant
cowgirl, dunghill-crazy
knees spread forever apart?

Self-hatred

Hate yourself, little girl
Ain't nobody gonna love you

If your hair is curly, straighten it
If your hair is straight, bleach it
If your hair is black, streak it
or ain't nobody gonna wait for you

When are you going to do
something with your hair?

The answer to all your problems
is in the right shampoo
alphabet balanced and
protein enriched
so you can hate yourself without it

Hate yourself, little girl
The industry is waiting for you
You're too flat and too skinny
You're way too plump
You look like a cow
Your breasts are all wrong
You need a running bra so you won't
jiggle as you jog

No one I know looks like Barbie
and even Marilyn couldn't
stand it when she did.

Cosmetic surgery just for you
unless you want to keep on hating.

Rag Rug

A virtual rag rug
which will never exist
except in her vision and mine

One with no floorboards creaking
underneath
No footsteps shuffling
it from place to place
No puppy curled in
lazy afternoon sleep

Yet for an instant
it *was*

as the string pieces,
biographical scraps from
a life-time spent among
fabrics,
fell from the storage bags,
lay unplanned and unfinished,
cut but unconnected
on a highly polished oak floor,
metaphors for all potentials
as yet unrealized
and often
unrealizable.

Panther

Sleek, shiny and art deco
it watched infant fingers
reaching for train tracks
as the Lionel Zephyr
rounded the curve
saw forests of Christmas
trees rise and fall,
dozens of Easter eggs
turn rainbow hues, then fade.

It greeted new bikes,
roller skates and Chevrolets,
witnessed first steps,
first dates, first kisses
first cousins at play.

A feline for all seasons,
it regarded episodes of Perry Mason
and Sundays of Ed Sullivan with
equal acritical aplomb.

It stood unchanging
through childhood's
facts and fantasies,
a palace guard
at the portal of
sacred memories.

Niece No More

I was born a niece
A daughter of course
but also a "sweet little niece."
Addie's niece and Edna's,
Ruby's, Nora's and Cleta's niece.
Annie, Emily, Cora in Montana,
Yes, their niece, too.

For sixty years
I have been
a niece.

Sororis filia,
Una sobrina, la nipote, la nièce.

Holiday cards and presents
from my aunts, my little aunties
the greetings and calls
the generosity, irreplaceable.
Role models, all.

The nurturing they represent,
the hand-made artistry,
the produce from their gardens
the harvest from their ovens.

The mothers of my cousins.

Now, after six decades,
a changed identity, mine.

Lamentable my place in the world
as non-niece.

Rest well,
aunties dearest.

Second Moment:

8:20 p.m.

Accident

Days I remember
like hot butter
before the promises melted
and the pavement curled
around the steel and the rubber

Hours glided easily
when everything fit

or at least functioned

before the soreness began and the
waiting

Nights, too, I remember
when sleep entered quickly
and took its solemn place
among the cells.

No longer.

Scars like visitors from
unchartered planets,
movements that shriek
at their own audacity
electric bruises that glow
across bones without memory
now calendar these days
between schizophrenic nights
that do battle with the intruder,
Pain.

Semi-Sacrifice

It was someone else they wanted
       the corolla heart to feed the savage stones
a virgin of the stature of Ixquic worthy of the spittle of Hunahpú
in whose hand to fashion two avengers for the strictly Mayan hell

       Gods out of fashion but not out of power

They examined me
       the butterfly patrol at the pyramids, iguanas by the side of
the well
       green lizard priests of an ancient order, the Quetzals in trees
at Uxmal

They watched me stroll
  the Paseo de la Muerte as though transfixed and climb the Sun
and Moon

My fear attracted them
       coagulated as the air at a blood-thick birth
They tested me and found me wanting, heart quivering
       constricted by loss of love, too thin for the divine banquet
       too yellow for holy consumption
skin falsely bronzed, unworthy of stretching on great ritual tambours
       of midnight importance
hair dark but not as black as a maiden's kiss of centuries' duration.

Imperfect sacrifice
       although it had begun

They left me scarred by the obsidian knife,
rejected by the Jaguar fates
crumpled
on the Mexican streets where Aztecs vanish at modern sounds
and Mayans linger no longer.

They regurgitated me
    after the first bite
and vomiting me back to reality
they vanished
on the siren-heavy night, from the pain-weary corridors, into the
pre-civilized dawn
to search
for a pure and more worthy victim.

X-Ray

I'm becoming a model
of pain.
I've tried it on now
for these months
and find that it fits
easily around the cartilage
snugly in the joints
tailor-made for the bone-marrow.

Parading down the ramp
with my cover girl grimace
showing the audience (smile)
the latest in fashions.

Notice how well it goes with crutches
(You can wear it anywhere
with a matching handbag).

It coordinates well with wheel chairs,
visits to hospitals,
the smell of dead flowers
and a jaunty beret.

Click-Click-Click

The photographs are finished.
Front-page stuff, you know.
Expert model.
Well-groomed PAIN.

Portrait

My photograph looks down
at my convalescent bed-self
from age twenty-three
when I must have been happy
bodily symmetrical
and unscarred.

Movement then was possible
though I sit perfectly still
focused
in my own kinetic energy.
I see it there,
the untiring motion
like David's hands...repose...
as I was taught by Michelangelo...
captured in the pre-bursting
moment
the pre-orgasmic second
the last splitting instant before the giant.

It has no shame
nor needs it
that ex-mirror
post-facto face,
the non-judgmental hair,
the lips that had never
formed pain sounds,
hollow moaning
beyond photographic
edges...

Framed there
watching its future.
why is there no horror,
no idea of Goliath?

Instead of rings
a sling shot
should have nestled
around my fingers
secure armor for the
tomorrows
that instead became
innumerable
crippled days.

Third Moment:

11:31 p.m.

Giza's Art

Giza
the master of transformations
Giza who converts trash to treasure
who challenges Einstein's concepts of space
and time
who relates to museums in the soul
who releases the art hidden in
a used tire, a rotten orange, a lost feather,
an empty bottle, a swatch of fabric
Giza who rearranges a canvas
a room, a life
who recreates a multiverse
Giza of the unfinished process
of unflagging energy
of the dynamic dance
Giza with flour on the floor
and paint on the face
in a perpetual motion of
excess, containment, flow.

Giza the howler or the sleeper
watching an internal video of revelation
Giza of colors, of shapes, of textures
of ears that are always cold.

Giza the quilter
or the sewer
Giza the builder
or the beguiled

Giza, child of the night.

Giza the seeker
of transcendence
of transmutation
of transmigrations of the spirit.

Giza of magic
and motion
and marvels.

Giza of light
and love
and longing.

Giza of sound
and spectacle
and synergy.

I now believe
I must believe
that this is but another
of your magical transformations,
a final artistic statement.

Giza the healer of others,
HEAL THYSELF

Giza's Studio

To enter a world
as a womb
where art is birthed,
a placenta place
of nurture and expectations
of wonder and delight
where miracles are as
common as cells
and twice as plentiful,
where dolls dance in the dark
and multiply by keening

To enter a space
as cluttered as a uterus
as sticky as blood
and as alive as oxygen
To enter with fire in the glance
to walk through walls
where existence means
living with art.

To enter a museum of the spirit
so active that sleep is
always on hold
for the encroaching hereafter
to enter a time as nonexistent
as the dinosaurs and of
twice their dimension
where dedication is omnipresent
and Einstein would
bow in awe,
where temporal reality means
living through art.

To enter a zone
of such sensorial power
that missiles explode
in the eyeballs and
resonate through
the bone marrow,
where existence is
summarized by
living around art.

To enter a galaxy
as immense as
a diaspora of emotion
where cultural entities
take up address
and a nucleus of atoms
swirls in atonement
where residence means
living art.

The House Across the River

A mother weeps
in the house across the river
for an absent son
who was never at home
in the house across the river
who could never paint
nor fuck nor love
in the house across the river
who could never dance
nor draw nor dream
in the house across the river.

The canvases on four walls
of the vacant room
proclaim Giza's space
but where is the life,
the essence, the energy?

A phantom wanders lost
in the bayou mists
and never knocks at the door of
the house across the river.

Of Fragile, Delicate Creatures

It is, you know
just one puff of smoke
just one brief encounter
just one mislaid microbe
which turns us
the masters of the universe
the geniuses of technology
the creators of art
inside out
from dominion over the earth
to a huddle of coughs
to a bundle of feeding tubes
to a breeding ground of disease.

It is, you know
an accident.

It is, you know
unplanned, untested.

We are, within the shells,
within the constructs
within the language
that protect us

merely delicate
merely fragile
merely creatures.

Invasions, 1991

Giza's body
a territory invaded
by a virus' heavy artillery,
by misplaced priorities
Germ warfare

Lungs as airless
as the sky above smoldering oil fields
a cerebral lining
as pitted as the roads to Baghdad,
veins mapping destruction
as surely as the video layouts
deep in the corridors of power.

Giza an artistic spirit
Iraq an ancient culture

Dust to dust
in deplorable waste.

The Dance

(for Giza)

Empty
The bed is empty

They came for you
to join the drumbeats in your heart
to meld with your rhythms
they came singly and in groups
to hold vigil
faces painted as warriors or lovers

They came to behold your gleaming skin
the perfect limbs
the mad gyrations

They came to spin and reel
to howl and whirl
in a dervish dance
of oblivion.

But they came
when the moon was full
just as you said they would.

The way it was s'posed to be

(for Giza)

We were s'posed to laugh
at final retrospectives
at the accumulation of pigments,
of memories, of conversions,
to recall the post-card days
of journeys
the live-in days arguing Alice Walker
until dawn
discussing, arguing
to begin again the vigil
over a full plate, an empty bottle
a palette of possibilities.

We were s'posed to be friends
for decades, centuries, eons
a wrinkle in the warp of time
as the multiverse sees it.

We were s'posed to contemplate
the daily joys, the yearly summations
to bullshit
to get drunk
to leave restaurants
staggering, to leave
the last millennium
gliding into this one
ready for encounters, openings, installations, recognition.

There are glasses of wine left
there are canvases empty
there are hearts, blistered
by events
but this is the way
it was s'posed to be.

Fourth Moment:

5:34 p.m.

Inter-species

We communicate
my dog and I
beyond the signifier
and Foucault
where the meanings of
tails and paws are deciphered,
in the realm where licking
the leg fresh-emerged
from the tub
means love.

On Driving My Dog To His Execution

Kidney failure.

Deliberations. Consternation. Ethical morass.
Decision.

Door closes.
Key in hand. It fits smoothly into the ignition.
Car starts. Accelerator, gas line, oil pump,
catalytic converter, cylinders, radiator,
tire pressure, brakes, suspension
All work smoothly.

Street lights, the punctuation marks of traffic,
conduct the semiotics
of mobility.

Car stops. Animal hospital.

It's all so normal
Yet not.

Leash, love, leash, love. Pull, push.
Cajole. Carry.

Enter. It's time. Finality.

Existentialism. Human hubris.
He didn't get to make the choice.

   It's euthanasia. It's execution.
   Both words start with an "e."

It's beyond grief.

Doggie At the Window

The car rounds the corner —

Noises perceptible to an evolved listener
waiting impatiently at the window,
alert to sounds out of range
for *homo sapiens*.

Ears perked, tail metronoming,
the bark of greeting,
the rush to the door.

Reunited, human and canine!

A glance at the window —

Where now that vision,
that anticipation of joy?

An ephemera
as fleeting as memory
as lasting as love.

My Imaginary Friend

Door scrapes on closing.

Leash taut in eager anticipation
as we bound down the steps

A bush, the garbage pail,
the new tree now half grown
planted when a puppy joined
the household,
our first stops.

Traffic light, wait.

Our park!

A squirrel to chase,
Another dog to greet,
A pat on the head
from a neighbor.

A realm rich in olfactory stimulation.
A territory marked, cherished
explored, loved.
A brisk pace interrupted
by frequent stops.

So much to inhale!

People gawk strangely.

They don't see that
I am walking my dog.

It is sunset;
I know that he is here.

Foto: April 1, 1994 – January 6, 2007

Searching the front page.

No headlines!

Devastating emptiness, unreported.
Water dish, untouched.
Leash hanging limp,
unused.

No headlines!
Not a mention!

An event that changes every moment
Something that aches so unceasingly
Unreported,
Unrecorded

Until now.

Fifth Moment:

6:00 a.m.

In Memoriam: Janis Joplin, October 4, 1970

Just ain't no hour
that isn't for Janis
the three-a.m. cosmic blues
on the clock
and all systems holding.
That dreadful moment before dawn
when you lie wishing
for one good man,
thinking maybe, just maybe
you'll try again, if not
tonight, then
sometime when there's a
half moon.

Buried alive in the sheets, in black satin,
in blues
you hope to hear
someone say
"Move over, baby"
cause he recognizes
a woman left lonely
ain't but half a woman
without her ball and chain.

The alarm clock rings in
the soul
I need a man to love
and there's still a little heart left for the taking,
piece by piece.

Noon and crying "Oh, Baby!"
work me lord, through
this day
cause I gotta get it,
Gotta get it while I can.

In Memoriam: Pablo Neruda, October 1973

Let me bow my head.

They said it was cancer
and they should know
military tumor
rattling in the long halls
cadaverous villains
parading in their mirrored
deformity
sending the official
coup-black limousine
to carry you to the gnawing grave.

It was so damn convenient.

Throw a poem
to save them
Throw an image
Throw a shadow
that cannot fade into
the Andean night.

You are, at last, a permanent
resident of the earth,
there to feed the coffin lining
with skin stretched
tight across the balding continent.

Plato de sangre.

Serve it to them
coagulated in their own violence
transfusion of
metaphors for
bent veins

dripping verbs, red,
and adjectives, red,
and subjects red and frenetic
Drop by drop.

Reconquer your
piece of the earth
wave poetry like a bastard flag
listen to the usurpers
grunt
because they won't understand.
Even in your most desperate song
you could not imagine this.

Twenty poems you engraved,
fifty, a million,
on the underneath
side of Chilean eyelids.

Don't let them wash away
as your people weep.

In Memoriam: Joe Strummer: 1952-2002

Was it London calling
or some unknown force
a kind of sadistic presence
inviting you to
the city of the dead?

Can 50 years ever be enough?

It was not a jolly holiday
to learn of your dying
during the days of fruitcake and eggnog
remembering you
and the many gifts you proffered
in your mere half century
as nomad and shocker.

You rocked us through
Reagan and raged as
we struck bargains with
the world
all lost in the supermarket
of our collective guilt.

You seared our brains
with Sandinista images
and Yankee dollar talk.

You railed at Capital Radio One,
the guns of Brixton and
Spanish bombs.

You wrote
You sang

You strummed
and it
mattered.

Where are you now that our
government has been ambushed
and the clampdown has escalated?

Where are you now to tell us that
"no kind of army
can hope to win a war
like trying to stop the rain
or still the lion's roar"?

Where are you now
John Graham Mellor
to raise our consciousness
to rock our sensibilities
to energize
to invigorate
to enlighten?

"Hate and war
the only things
we got today"
and we need
YOU!

You left us way
        too young
You left us way
        too soon
You left us waiting
      waiting
              forever waiting

for a ninth night
at Bond's.

(For Miguel)

Carolyn G. Heilbrun: Dead at Age 77

Dear Carolyn,
You answered the question
posited by Camus
and you responded brilliantly
as you did
to all of life's deep queries.

Sylvia's choice was not yours…
more Maude
and a ring flung into the waves
of a future in which you chose
not to participate.

A decision, yes, that reaffirms you,
the woman, the scholar, the writer,
our Amanda Cross.

What would we have done
without you,
we with feet in academia,
hearts in the world
and noses in the pages of Nancy Drew?

Liminality
is now yours
because it's
the final transition.

How I wish you
transcendence
and a chalice as full
as an afterlife.

Thank you for existing,
for leading, for inspiring
for we are naught
but followers
on such a trail
as yours.

In Memoriam: Edward Said: 1935-2003

You picked an inappropriate time to leave us,
as though there were ever an
opportune moment for ending a
life as full and complex as yours

But now? Why now, when we need
you most desperately?

Who else can challenge us to think beyond boundaries,
to explore deeply what Fox News ignores?

Who else can quote widely from texts
as old as civilization itself
and ask us to interrogate anachronistic rivalries?

Who else can stimulate us
to question those who hijacked
our government for
imperialistic quests?

Who but you, Edward Said,
linguist and author,
professor and Palestinian,
exile, New Yorker and citizen of the world,
can bring us to our senses
as we face ancient tendencies
for domination backed by
horrific modern technologies?

Who, Edward Said, who?

As we mourn your passing
we thank you humbly for
moving among us
an intellectual king of the Orient,
our star of Bethlehem.

In Memoriam: Octavia Butler: (1947-2006)

Are you now Earthseed
dispersing your talented DNA
throughout the galaxies
of your imagination?

Are you kindred spirit or fledgling?

Do you continue to exist
in the interstices of change,
between now and forever,
then and now and nowhere,
inhabiting the eternal limen?

You sowed your parables,
trickster that you are,
on fertile ground.

Your acorn grows
in the minds
of your bereaved readers.

Death, after all, is but
an adulthood rite.

Hiroshima: Exculpation

I was gestating
safe in the womb
when the egg turned
and the universe shook.

My amniotic conscience was clear
while the past was obliterated
on the shores of the distant Nipponese sea
and the present obstructed
in the camps here.

Was my umbilical cord
connected to these madmen?

Expelled at last
to live with their hubris
to adjust to the shift
to the horror,
for the balance of history
did not die
with the dinosaurs
and I was not birthed into a void.

Chilean Obituary: The Other September 11

    for Pedro Pietri

A quiet reigns…
whispers, tiptoeing,
reverance…
A child lays
a rose at the base
of the marble slabs
Identities engraved in blood
rows and rows of them
reeking of tortures unnamable.

Disappeared.
Snatched from among us.
More than 3,000 of them.

Sobs escape from
blocked throats of grandmothers,
sisters, brothers, friends.

A generation is missing!

I stand with mourners,
the culpability of my passport
throbbing in my pocket
for before the planes and
the towers, before
the ash and the rubble,
long before there was
"nine eleven"

there were democratic elections and Popular Unity

There was Juan, a truck driver
There was Miguel, a worker in the Copper Mine
There was Milagros, a university student
There was Olga, a journalist
There was Manuel, a farmer
There was Salvador Allende, victorious,
in the Moneda Palace.

There was the Cold War
spreading fear in Washington

There was Nixon
There was Kissinger

There was the CIA

On the other September 11
there were helicopters
and coup-black limousines
There were tanks and artillery
and Allende
in his pathetic helmet

It was 1973.

Where were you?
Where was I?
Where was the horror when
Pinochet hijacked his nation
and butchered
Juan
Miguel
Milagros
Olga and
Manuel?

Juan, age 28
Miguel, age 33
Milagros, age 24
Olga, age 17
Manuel, age 19

Now in Chile
there is a monument
They can mention
these names,
restore to them their history
bemoan that
fateful September day
when terror overtook
the streets of Santiago
and Juan, Miguel,
Milagros, Olga,
Manuel, Cecilia,
Rosita, Carlos, Pablo, Luis, Margarita
Isabel, Jorge, Ramón, Cesár, Jesús
and their comrades began

to disappear
Forever.

On a Clear Day…

On a clear day
you could see

On a clear day, the Jersey
swamplands stretched
to suburbs humming

On a clear day bridges connected,
dissected and reflected
the human hunger
for crossing over

On a clear day
the South Bronx stood
amidst its social rubble

On a clear day
Queens raced,
Brooklyn breathed,
Staten Island cruised
Into the new century

On a clear day,
Manhattan,
Oh, Manhattan…

On a clear day
the engineering marvel
dwarfed hominid ants and
matchbox cars

On a clear day
dinner proffered
a window on the world

On a clear day
envious skyscrapers
paid homage to window washers,
lawyers, bankers, waiters, executives,
housekeepers, vendors, secretaries,
managers, middle managers, CEO's,
janitors, programmers, analysts, gofers,
chefs,
and security guards

On a clear day
The planes struck
The smoke rose
The steel melted
The ash tumbled

And there was no more
clarity
There was no more

Icarus, September 12

It's 6:00 a.m. and the hour
of Icarus
Daedalus summons his laggard
son

There is a solemn silence
In the skies

An absence

The avian imitators
give way to turtle doves
grosbeaks
ravens

Icarus slumbers

Gulls circle, screeching

Listening, longing, yearning for normalcy
Ears on high alert
Eyes tuned to the dawn

Yet Icarus dozes on

A military jet slices the
silence

Morning dressed in blood
becomes mourning

Icarus, wounded,
remains
grounded.

Islands

Islands intrigue
Islands intoxicate

At once deceptively knowable
and unknown,
their brine-bathed margins
set limits
define infinity.

Beaches and shorelines
Harbors and bays
Coves and piers and marinas,
endless horizons.

Islands determine
what is accessible,
what is beyond reach

Islands liberate
and imprison
Islands enlighten
and infuriate

Islands isolate

Islands bestow
and take away.

Insularity becomes
a mode of living,
a locus for dying.

Memorial, March 2002

Diffuse, intangible, reaching
for definition
two beams mark
the locus of our grief.
We want them back,
no, we need them back.
The mauve reflections from
an early morning ferry ride,
the golden dazzle of late
afternoons from the Turnpike,
the luminous presence on clear nights
orienting our movements
around the City.
Our incomplete skyline
suffers, as we do,
the inconceivable loss,
the immeasurable sadness,
the emptiness in
our bones.

"Remember,
Reflect,
Rebuild"
Twin spires of
peaceful aspirations.

When? 2007

I look
my eyes prowl the horizon
my sense of aesthetics craves its visual anchor
my New York self aches with nostalgia

There is a hole in the sky

Six years.
Nothing. Nada. Zip.
Zero.

My city needs a compass
my state a marker
my nation, a mission
my planet, salvation

I need the twins

Beacons, targets
symbols of grace, power
and evil

I need their physicality
their concrete, steel and glass
that one day
turned to ash
signifying
innocence lost

seemingly forever.

Sixth Moment:

3:00 a.m.

Poem as…..

I

Poem as ivy,
as poisonous itching
beneath the skin
as red blotches
and patches of
dubious origin.

Poem as leprous sorcery
as swollen pink eyes,
as contagion and fear
of solitude
of calamine stench
and rumpled sheets
as a summer hazard
that knows no
calendar, that
creeps epidermally
in winter, in spring,
an epidemic.

Poem as unavoidable
attack,
as unplanned
scratching, as broken nails
exhausted raw skin.

II

Poem as estrus,
as genitalia quickening
to a drum beat
in the blood,
as menstrual, post
and pre, as red words

bleeding onto
a pristine page.

Poem as fecundity,
the period awaited,
the cycle in motion
the thump of verb against
object, of nouns
in the cells
the desire in
the marrow,
the blur of bones.

III

Poem as survival
as weapon against the
encroaching night
as necessity
as absent lover
as creative ink
to pour into an orifice
on hold,
wadded paper throbbing to a
verbal orgasm.
Poem as balm
because restlessness
needs antidote
as fulfillment
as approach
to a problem so old
that to mention it is
primordial cliché.
Poem as existence
as seducer and nightmare

as the 3 a.m. word
that seeks victim and release
as activity so consuming
that alternatives
are non
existent.

Cats

My syllables are
3 a.m. cats
in heat beneath
the March-dark window.

From under the cars
they come
fear-smeared offerings
on the oil-dripped pavement.

No one announced this screaming convocation.
Yet no indecent feline is absent.

They vote, prowl, hunt,
arch, ache, and annoy me
(even more than others)
with their endless furry processions
of unconquerable desire.

They attack occasionally in
fits of desperation
inky with
howling, screeching vowels.

Windows open. Objects fly
at the gawky gathering.

They retreat into the night
heavy with sex and
expectation.

They await,
smug in their
battery-eyed
claw-sharp irreality

ready to
realign,
reassemble,
parade uninvited
across still another
3 a.m. page.

My Voice

My voice conjugates itself
at dawn
between plant leaves and dark sponges
and moments like electric knives.
My whisper leaves imperceptible trails
of lazy phosphorescence
heavy on a summer madness.
My voice destroys me,
disobeys me,
follows rhythms from other times,
spreads grease where fingerprints
would rather design a new tale.
I invite it back into my larynx
(but it listens only to itself
and no longer heeds my commands).
My hollow throat,
my empty, sordid gargle,
my words like lozenges
that no longer soothe.

My underlip is numb
as the morning star wanders
back into its stable.

Passion As…

I

Passion as transfusion
as blood bursts
calling cellular armies
into action,
as capillary invasion, occupation
domination of self by
other self
through needle sharp pain
stinging bruises
collapsed veins
measuring out sustenance
and survival
milliliter by
millidrop.

II

Passion as horned bull
as armed matador
facing off in a
death dance
of ritualistic origin
as antique as Minos
and just as bloody
upon the sand.

III

Passion as labyrinth
unchartered by Greek deities
unexplored by Borges
uncluttered by
double axes,

a territory so nebulous
that even the Minotaur
cannot escape
nor give instruction as you
leap to ride
the mythical beast.

Poem Without Face

Naked, hairless and unrhymed
it sits
wearing, on isometric occasions,
a body without shadows
and always, always earrings.

It springs to meet tomorrow
between shudders, ribbon-black and
haunted
in a Styrofoam case.

On jaunty afternoons,
rare,
it unmasks
noun by verb the
heavy make-up,
dimmer dreams,
alien triads of imperfection.

What happened between
the milk-glass mornings,
the bitter-stained pillows?

Eyes weep red
for the no-face poem
for the no-poem face.

Pastime

Poetry is desperation
the alarm clock that
goes off in the tongue
the ledge between nightmares
and reality
the tightrope without a net
a lion jumping through the
ring of fire
sweaty palms reaching for
an elusive trapeze.

It enters respirators
at the choking moment
and is there lurking
between flesh and the
ever-threatening blade.

Poetry is the instant
before the jump
always one step this side
of eternity.

There are no second chances
for those who worship severely
savage gods.

"FreAk ShoW. Step right up!"

Prose, a more constant companion,
deals its game
in daytime
stalks among the people
requires no deformity.

Nocturne

The witches whine and wail.
What are the magic incantations?
I beg them from nonexistence
to appear like Banquo's ghost
before this sleepless usurper.

I worship at the source
of inspiration
divine or alien,
it matters little,
female or phallic,
unimportant,
muse or amusing
or heavy midnight apparition.

What is wrong with my
burnt offerings?

Somnambulist with pen
I cannot wash the ink
from these poor hands.
Out, out damn spot
I hear the Lady crying.

The dagger entered
gouging unfettered syllables
from their bloody repose.
Poetry dies in its
royal castle.

There is a knocking at hell's gate
as morning conquers like Macduff.

Photography As…

Photo as revelation
of self in light
as soul expressed, as body probed
as Narcissus reveling
in his own image
as "experience captured"
by bombardments of energy
the conversion of object
into colors, dots, images in
shades of gray
the transmigration of spirit
as act of voodoo
and taboo
as possession
as cultural totem

Photo as alchemy
as emergence
as birth and afterbirth
as a dark voyeurism
of adrenalin and chemistry
beyond the expected product of
a magus
waving wands

Photo as icon
as aesthetic problem
as evidence of reality
or irreality, or
nature or aberration.

Photo as interpretation
as vision or quest
as omnipresent as history
and twice as dangerous.

Visitation

Deities descend
but not always in showers
of golden rain.

You say it is vanity
yet Hellenic initiates know
that Apollo comes on
a rape of rays
that bursts between spread legs
that enters open pores impregnating
all with miracle heat
to melt the lingering frost
of a winter's hibernation.

Deities visit
and I arch my back
to form an altar
for their worship.

Habitat

Where I reside is a world
of syntax, not taxes
of images and imagination,
a world of metaphor
   simile
   synecdoche
   denouement
   climax
and resolution,
open pages of prefaces, preambles
prologues, protagonists, plots.

The world in which I claim citizenship
has covers
   has bindings, not artificial borders
   has narrative structure, not loss,
   has agency, not greed
though avarice is a Silas Marner theme

My world is authored, written, designed
unlike nature's total indifference

My world is dark squiggles
on a bright page
   fonts and fantasy
   press and predestination
   marketing and magic
   capitalism and culture

My world
My hybrid world
My only sword against despair,
against oblivion.

Sailing To You....

I sail to you as to a cove of love

the clouds moving swiftly
buffeted by breezes in
atmospheric levels
we can't imagine

The raindrops falling angularly
swept by tides in
oceanic upheavals
we can't fathom

The lightning striking anonymously
guided by forces in
terrestrial fields
we can't measure

My love

My nimbus
My sustenance
My energy

My sunlight…

My snug harbor

(For Miguel)

About the Author

Marilyn Kiss teaches language and literature classes at Wagner College, Staten Island, New York, where she also coordinates the study abroad program. After growing up in rural Missouri, she moved to the East Coast during the "Summer of Love" and has left only to travel widely or to spend time in Spanish-speaking countries. She and her long-time companion, Miguel Angel, are avid photographers, cinephiles, peace activists, and vegetarians who love animals.

As the bumper sticker says, she would much rather be reading.

www.ingramcontent.com/pod-product-compliance
Lightning Source LLC
Chambersburg PA
CBHW071020080526
44587CB00015B/2435